How to Cast a Beautiful Animal

POETIC JUSTICE INSTITUTE

Elisabeth Frost, *series editor*

How to Cast a Beautiful Animal

Diana Keren Lee

Fordham University Press New York 2026

Copyright © 2026 Fordham University Press

All rights reserved. No part of this publication may be reproduced, stored in a retrieval system, or transmitted in any form or by any means—electronic, mechanical, photocopy, recording, or any other—except for brief quotations in printed reviews, without the prior permission of the publisher.

Fordham University Press has no responsibility for the persistence or accuracy of URLs for external or third-party Internet websites referred to in this publication and does not guarantee that any content on such websites is, or will remain, accurate or appropriate.

Fordham University Press also publishes its books in a variety of electronic formats. Some content that appears in print may not be available in electronic books.

Visit us online at www.fordhampress.com.

For EU safety / GPSR concerns: Mare Nostrum Group B.V., Doelen 72, 4831 GR Breda, The Netherlands, gpsr@mare-nostrum.co.uk

Library of Congress Cataloging-in-Publication Data available online at https://catalog.loc.gov.

Printed in the United States of America

27 26 25   5 4 3 2 1

First edition

Contents

Season 2

Season 3

Season 4

How to Cast a Beautiful Animal

Season 1

American Anagrams

In my cinema,
life begins and ends
with a letter.
The ice cream,
the car, the camera.
In between:
crime, the man,
arms in the air.
A name and a race.
In the dream,
something's missing.
(Can I get an amen?)
Still, I eat the rice.
Still, I aim to be near.

The One

the one river
by the one mountain
which resembles the wound
the one grievance grown up
that no one can climb

one mushroom
on the last tree
breathing one leaf
on the branch extended
for anyone who will notice

you drive down the street
with a gallon left
go to the only bar in town
find one stool, have one beer
meet the person

who will listen with one ear
tilted to your only secret
the same repeated season
which is also your sole
excuse for living this life

singular song of praise and lament
so many tones rolled into one
note for your final night
a fork and a knife
lying side by side on the table

First Language

After years of speech, it occurred to me: Did I love one language more than another?

English, I was faithful to you, your verbs and prepositions.

(That spring, having placed my soul on a bike seat at the edge of morning,
beneath a too small sky.)

But I always kept Korean somewhere, even if it felt forgotten, like all my body parts:
lungs, the heart always connected to the breath. Certain words more than others.

Spirals I Have Admired

> *The Italian philosopher Vico had this theory that time moves more in a spiral than it does in a line. He believes that's why we repeat ourselves, including our tragedies, and that if we are more faithful to this movement, we can move away from the epicenter through distance and time, but we have to confront it every time.*
>
> —Ocean Vuong

shell of a snail,

mouth opening as it goes inside

the hard curl of a telephone cord

(slip your fingers in the spaces between)

announcing the newborn

the whorl of her hair

scent of a rose and its swirl

thumb pressed to the page to identify you

and all the dreams that surround you

as you fill in the bubble of the test question

then erase it after you second-guess

loop of mixtape my brother gave me

when I was younger when we still talked

now tangled somewhere in a landfill

with a rolled-up tube of retinol

like a limp party horn

thin strip of voicemail in which my dad

said I love you, the way he held my hand

like a tiny shell in the florets of the sun

frog's tongue catching its prey

as we push language from our mouths

our stubborn words returning to us

as they ring in our ears

yoga mat waiting to be unfurled

ink flowing from the tip of a pen

while the clock repeats itself

the cursive *O*

whirlpool of Korean spa in which I sit with my mother

space between us the length of an orange rind

unpeeled in one piece

a pause a comma never stopping

twisting until the end of time

[In the scenes from my childhood]

In the scenes from my childhood, all the animals are beautiful. The trees are swaying and I am pretending to be sad. At church the girls smile through their teeth, whisper *oh god* in their ears newly pierced with the brightest bling of their lives. There is murmuring, there is prayer. There is a scene that is blurry that I am trying to remember. My mother close-up, the glamour in her grammar. *Please write this one day.* In my monologue at the end, I convey many emotions, even the ones I can't name.

Neighborhood Watch

green flowers of CorningWare dishes
bordering the boredom of poverty
kimchi jars the weight of babies
canned laughter of sitcoms
and the rest of the block
who didn't look like you
through divided curtains
their front lawns not like
the toilet paper hanging
from branches like ghosts
rolls of unprinted receipts
trains of unwanted brides
not like the scrolls of angels
with everything wished for
the smashed car window
white as snow on the ground
now glittering in an afterlife
your Korean-born brothers
on opposite sides of the couch
watching at full volume
door open to the backyard
born in the USA I was
in war-torn jeans
then and now

Self-Portrait as Asian American Actress

In high school plays, I was remembered for my roles as a man and animal.
Dressing like a boy kept me from being mistaken for a prostitute or a ghost.

My Brother Was My Father

My brother was my father, my mother was my daughter, and my father was, well, the father. Obey the father and God, Heaven and hell—what's the difference when it will never end? I was both praised and blamed in Korean words I can't say, but I didn't understand the difference: attention is always paid to the favorite, especially when she is a girl with intelligence and rage. On my seventeenth birthday, my brother told me not to be a fuckup like he was, then called me one, years later, over the holidays. *Wasn't everything your fault?* The last time I spoke with him, I gave him *The Corrections* for Christmas. I considered replacing the C with a K. When I asked a friend why he would treat me this way, he said, *It's pretty obvious to me. He wants what he can't have.* But every unhappy family is happy in its own way too, my mother's flowers circling the house. We made it to the woods, where brother and sister are translated as mother and daughter, where we are still walking.

Ode to the '90s

mist of rhythm guitar and dial-up
off the grid   punk rap plaid
radio cranked up like the sun
machine or actual drums
my angst is still young
and highly flammable
something interrupted
meant to be read out of order
one chord change to another
feels like a lifetime like
doors creaking on their hinges
mosh pit melting pot
stock photography model
crying in movie theaters
femme fatale escapes
flames or extinguishes them
makes you feel   a rose growing
take a picture   fast as you can
does the toxic green in music videos
mimic mountain dew or the shade

of trembling leaves
the economy
a woman
a woman I said
song fading slowly like daybreak

Country Dinner Playhouse

It is the end of the seventies,
the beginning of his life in America.
In his white shirt and black bow tie

fanned like a giant butterfly,
the tallest Asian you've ever seen,
my father looks more like a movie star

than a busboy or an extra. Hair wavy
smoke from a cowboy's cigarette,
grin blinding like the stack of plates

cleared between the Oak Ridge Boys
and Johnny Cash, bright lights
trailing him for three years.

In the Polaroid, the man laughing
with him—an entertainer?
What was the joke he'd just told?

He can't say. I flip the photo over.
Instead of a date, a black screen
surrounded by a white frame.

A coworker's face burned by hot oil
thrown out on the street. At night
my father brought leftovers home.

Ferment

Red chili pepper/fish sauce/ginger/sea salt/green onion stain on denim.
Radish peeled then sliced on a mandoline like a diving board,
flames in a silver bowl. Don't try this at home, Umma said.
Too much work—easier to buy.
Garlic pounded with mortar and pestle, cases closed.
In my mother's country, clay pots in the snow like coffins.
Unearthed from the back of my refrigerator, the smell reminds me.

1984

on the employee-discounted PC Junior
we played the OG King's Quest

the prince retrieving an egg from a pixelated nest
in big blue sky

dad's fingerprint on the microchip
silicon cilia surrounded by golf course green

blueprint of a village
big brother   latchkey kid watching me

dad loaded boxes   bent his knees   used his core

the prince falling down a hole in the floor of the shack

memory boards   all he manufactured
tiny silver pins writing the future   soon to be obsolete

the prince eating a mushroom

the prince drowning in a rushing river

as I type these words   packed into the hard drive

what can only be seen if you break the thing open

the piggy bank full of quarters

processing all the circuitous paths
the logic in how we got from there to here

Self-Portrait as Asian American Actress

Red lips, red dress,
I light a cigarette
by craft services

as the rest of the cast
continues filming.
Phone on silent,

I filter myself
black and white.
I am almost

a star.
Yellow sun
for days

becomes me
and I almost
become a cloud

pushed out by
night's curtains.
I repeat *Yes*,

the one line
given to me.
With a bill thin

as the last page
of a script,
I enter the cinema.

The projector's
tongue unravels,
erases itself.

Like how I imagine
my black hair all over
the cutting room floor.

Self-Portrait as Asian American Actress

~~Red lips, red dress,~~
I light ~~a cigarette~~
~~by craft services~~

~~as the rest of the cast~~
~~continues filming.~~
~~Phone on silent,~~

~~I filter~~ myself
~~black and white.~~
~~I am almost~~

~~a star.~~
Yellow ~~sun~~
~~for days~~

~~becomes me~~
~~and I almost~~
~~become a~~ cloud

push~~ed out by~~
~~night's curtains.~~
~~I~~ repeat ~~*Yes,*~~

~~the one line~~
~~given to me.~~
~~With a bill thin~~

~~as the last page~~
~~of a script,~~
~~I enter the cinema.~~

~~The projector's~~
~~tongue unravels,~~
~~erases itself.~~

~~Like how I imagine~~
~~my black hair all over~~
~~the cutting room floor.~~

Naming These Things

I've had it up to here with difficulty.
This level of nonsense can't be seen

but God can't be, either.
Give him new clothes and a makeover.

He can sit in a café and predict
the order will be right.

How many times can you get it wrong?
The options: eggs, bagel, stalemate.

Let's reconvene when I get to the hole—
that is, when it's eaten whole.

Deposition is not a proposition
and tomatoes are fruit, though they don't

need to be classified. Perhaps the famous
poet named his book *Some Trees*

because some, not all, were saved.
There is room for another king or queen.

If only you could remember the game,
the process of naming these things.

Season 2

Trip

All my life I've carried a suitcase I could never fully open.
Poems filled with baggage, luggage filled with words.

Where Are You From?

Where are you from?
A country that has forgotten its name.

Where do you live?
A city that has lost its outrage.

What do you do?
I hand out samples labeled as hope in empty cups.

What brought you here?
The blue sea, the blue sky.

Where are you from?
How many miles from Isla Mujeres to Jeju-do?

Haenyeo of Jeju Island

Biosphere reserve
in my mother's country:
fields of rapeseed, azaleas,
cones of a dormant volcano.

Elderly women in black rubber
dive, brave the cold sea together
without gear, rise from the depths
with clams, abalone, and mackerel.

In a parking lot across from bulldozers,
protesters against a planned naval base
pass around tangerines peeled like embryos
as tourists visit not for the mass graves

but for honeymoons, museums of teddy bears,
chocolate, and sex. When I think of Korea
I think of war and religion, resistance

and ritual, grandmothers and mothers
asking if we've eaten, green-black
sheets of seaweed like newsprint.

Lines of breath sung from the water
with strong legs, strong lungs,
shamans a bridge to the wind.

Artemisia

Wormwood: the Korean acupuncture cure-all,[1] mounds rolled and placed on hands, the back. Burned like tiny volcanoes. Species of *Artemisia*, also used in many other countries, to ease the stomach. Mugwort, sagebrush. For Koreans, people who consume army stew, a temporary cure for *han*,[2] quelling the heart. The last time my mother visited me in New York, she brought some in a black plastic bag checked in through LaGuardia, my father saying be careful, might be mistaken for marijuana. When they left, I untied the bag and placed the herbs—the *sook*—in the lacquered bowl they gave me. Tried smoking it, but no effect. It stayed in my hair the next day like a lover's scent on my pillow. My mother left a pair of green socks behind, reminding me how as a child I once smelled her feet as she took a nap, sensing that she was a woman used to standing. When she was a child, they said she would never walk.

1. My maternal grandparents were acupuncture doctors, and my grandmother was among the first women to practice.

2. Han: no exact translation, but often compared to sorrow, regret. Another definition of wormwood is "a state or source of bitterness or grief."

Lessons in Korean

the geometry of Hangul

vowels and consonants

a rising and falling

of lines, of circles

the sides of a square

I am syllabic, I am divided

by sight, by sound

I can speak, but I speak slowly

constructing a puzzle

I am Altaic

I am mountainous

the narrative does not end

but there will not always be

time to search for words

that once burned

Han

With no English equivalent,
a concept rather than emotion

though we are full of—
cousin of duende, of soul—

Give me your oppression,
your resentment, bitterness

of roots in the ground,
the sparrow's sorrow.

The news delivered as sermon.
The sparrow on the ground.

It does not seek vengeance
yet yearns for it.

A lover, a country.
Blood in the gut.
Amends tomorrow.

grief

green feeling
tucked under
then up
e.g., fig tree

filigree:
easy reeling
i.e., a ring
and he flees

fires, reefs

Anniversary

A phone hangs on its cord,
listens to the wind.
I will not cross the bridge
looking for remorse.
I will not call—like the dead
you do not need a lecture.
The trees, in the meantime,
practice their golden rule.

Land of the Morning Calm

Three and a half decades after the war,
we searched for skyscrapers, taxis, palaces.
Saw a man pissing at the end of a road at dusk,

blue accruing to peach then dissolving to black.
Our parents our tour guides,
I wondered about their lives, and mine:

had I been born there, had I never been born
with the urge to speak, of what they carried,
what I translated from their faces.

The car approaching the mountain,
the first I had ever seen—
later I came to know *mountain after mountain,*

the Korean proverb *san neomeo san.*
Haitians say *Dèyè mòn, gen mòn.*
Beyond mountains, there are mountains.

An Unfinished History

the Russian guard paused
and let my aunt cross
she looks like my daughter

this could have been now
you could have been
a soldier, mother

singing for an army
for her childhood
the canned food

out of place and yet
vital to this scene
not the last

*

serrated edges of
green perilla leaves
black rice
in the bag like fleas

*

my father wore his first pair
of jeans on Labor Day

in the years before citizenship
they called him John Wayne
(stoic Korean or ugly American?)
handsome, strong enough to kill

*

Vienna sausage or tuna
eating on all fours like a cat
pretending, anywhere but here

*

the first pop song
I memorized:
learning to love yourself
it is the greatest love of all

*

my mother watching Oprah
remembers *The Color Purple*
which I still haven't seen

Korean drama
you think I said trauma

*

my mother loved her father
and her mother country

my mother wanted to go back
my father wanted to stay

*

violets on the windowsill

*

after 9/11
I took two suitcases to New York
in the rush of red-eye
I passed the gate

my parents could not cross
the guard did not budge

my father, unable to embrace:
sir, do you have a daughter

*

when I was young I asked my father
what happened to his hands
swollen like branches

he said when he was an infant
he reached for the fire

and I get the sense
this isn't the story

*

a dictator here,
a dictator there

*

my mother says warmly
after her friend's son's funeral:
promise never to kill yourself

and often:
enjoy your life

*

my father dreams
she and I are walking
in another country

red flowers
for a hundred days

Season 3

Say Something About Yourself

—after OK Cupid quizzes

I'm warm, often deadpan.
Or a lively hotpan.
One less car, one more poet.
I've never been with a poet
but if that were to ever
happen, I'd like to press
my poems against their poems
one of my lines, one of theirs
and then mine again, fingers
laced like a CEO twiddling
his thumbs over a window
with a view of the water.
Libra Leo Cancer,
I consult my parents
but go my own way.
On a typical Friday night
I'm atypically hot. I smell
nice, I've been told.
I'll try anything once.
Do you like to argue?
Yes, the best part

is making up.
Are you happy with your life?
That's a really long poem
I'm trying to write.

Two Suitcases and a Map

how many degrees
to the center of everything
said someone famous

a rat claws its way
out of the heap

now there's a 7-Eleven
on Eleventh and Seventh

and farther east

a man with bagpipes
picking up static

the last of yesterday's news
on the ground

jazz runs through the trees
smashed in the street

chords of stoplights
ringing in the leaves

green, gold, red   again and again

in the park

—everyone and their solo

on your way to a table for one
(table for three
the couple arguing)

subway   typewriter   rain

Fortune Favors the Patient

We played the same role
in different films
and no one could decide
whose performance was better.
The screenplay a spool of fortunes
from the world's gigantic cookie:
Your optimism will lead
to great success. The first thing
to look for in a problem is its
positive side. Old age is always
20 years older than you are.
So of course I walked slowly
pretended the camera wasn't there.
I did my own hair
and carried all my luggage
filled with unfinished poems.
Everything was filmed in one take.

At the Wheel

Instead of a needle, a wooden wheel

certain in my cycle as a captain, a bachelor at sea

Instead of fawning over someone

I've got a mouth full of yarn

I weave rugs so I can sweep things under them

buy sweatpants online   delivered in a brown box

I don't play solitaire — too many ranks and numbers

my favorite game was Old Maid, remembering

all the pairs and getting them squared away

but that maid   I pitied and envied her, not having to deal

with anyone — in her aloneness she was special, the last one left

I quit Tinder to spend the night with *Great Expectations*

I was a spinster before it was hip — how I miss

rotary phones, numbers coming back to where they started

my parents pray every day for me to get married

no pressure of course, just a positive spin

which runs in the family   keeps things going

Self-Portrait as Asian American Actress

I'm not a doctor or a robot.
I just play one on TV.

Take one, take two.
Margaret Cho, Lucy Liu.

Neither happy nor sad,
neither she nor you.

When in doubt
cast the couch,

turn the screw.
If not for my laziness

I'd be a concert pianist.
Keys straight like teeth.

If mine were white
would I be famous?

If it were a race, then—
if not now, when?

Pearl & Ash

I am more than dried Artemisia
in wooden compartments.
I am fluent in spices, and he
knows how to fill in the blanks.
Low light complements
the thrum around our table,
evening warming up.
As he tells me what he has held
his mouth reminds me of pears,
the window's tangle of trees.
He asks for more water,
skirts the steak poached for days.
We await the sweetness of fish,
pluck of bones as the bottles
throb with chilies and ginger,
breath caramelized.
I finally feed him,
wildly tender and tea-cured.

Office Sun

sky nearly as blue
as computer screen
river's ribbon of ink
printing us from the ferry
and faxing us back
sun punching holes
through the bar
chart of trees
newly looseleaf
condos stapled together
to the clouds stacked white
and idle as blank sheets
air laying us off
from death every day
and asking us back
with reduced benefit
multimillion green
office stamped on
the ground pad
with all its bugs
to be shut down
and continued
sky nearly as black
as computer screen

Walking in Koreatown, Los Angeles

After H Mart I take my friend to R Bar
where the password to get in isn't gentrification
but we know all the answers to this trivia
across from the half-empty Salvadoran restaurant
lunch and dinner scrolling across in neon Hangul
intergenerational trauma: almost iambic pentameter
which can't be cured with a little white pill
but I wouldn't know because I've never tried

Instead of a drink I'll take a full moon, better music
and diplomacy, say anger is another person
sing Prince and Cocteau Twins karaoke
and call you when you're back in Harlem
the time it would take to fly if I could
with everyone who has ever asked
where I'm from and where I'm going
take a walk until I reach Hollywood
where the foreign languages end
and the marvelous sun gets credit

I Realize I Need New Music

Fine line between boredom and restlessness.
An extra syllable the sea washes ashore,
what the sound of cars is mistaken for.

The bus is stalled on Sunset
date and time scrolling above us.
I rise to give the elderly woman a seat.

The old music on my old phone
shuffles to the middle of the album
earbuds branching like a wishbone.

Halfway through the song I wonder,
Would it be better first or last instead?
Or does the order not matter?

Years ago, a new friend said he'd believe me
if I said I listened to any kind of music
whatever the answer.

A song is a kind of patience,
getting to something, and somewhere.
When I finally arrive home

I remove my headphones
to hear the refrigerator, crickets,
the wind through the trees.

Self-Portrait as Asian American Actress

In the city of angels, I play Medusa
mistaken for palm tree,

featured extra, tourist #3.

On Halloween I'm Bruce Lee,
disarm the room with one-liners.

In my dreams, I break the screen
into hundreds of separate screens

like the scales of a glass dragon,
red dress into drops of blood.

I write a script in which I live
until the end, to be continued.

And when the silence continues,

I dive into a pool so blue
I can't see my reflection.

Insta Sonnet

On a merry-go-round of stories
I scroll past major award winners,
this season's fashion, young gizzard shad.
Tiny red carpets set ablaze by fire emojis,
trees unscreened in the distance
in reverse chronological order.
The kids and their kitsch, recycled air.
The camera-ready ads follow me to sleep
and listen to my dreams, even the ones
that don't make money or sense.
A subway station that never ends.
A cat wears a shirt of a cat in a shirt
and the death toll keeps rising.
A robot says *art* like it has a heart.

In the Morning Light

Cyndi Lauper in the living room,
my mother cooking liver in the kitchen.
I was staring at the sky through the blinds.

At five and six and seven, the song again
during laps in gym class, pausing a second
before running counterclockwise.

Knowing that being a girl was temporary
but I would remember the empty stage
we ran toward and away from.

The phone never ringing,
the moon hiding its lover
the sun even from itself—

at least someone got to walk in it.
A woman lies on the sand.
Mama, who never wanted

a husband, only to climb
mountains and more mountains,
married my poor father.

All those years in a line.
Her once beautiful hands
weathered like maps folded

over and over again,
polishing artificial hearts
of their grit until they shined.

She saved her worries
for the middle of the night.
In the middle of my life

at the end of our call
she tells me to enjoy life,
to have fun.

Living Alone

An ant crawling across my keyboard: Are there others?
Shaped like an ear, the question mark takes up so much space.
How do you meet people? I ask having lasted this long knowing
the answer, by joining a club that would have me as a member.
I get a drink at the bar, stools to my left and right ellipses
waiting to be filled. Everything's dependent on something.
Day and night, the pause of long lines, stop signs,
the drama of sunset, which is free and never fails.
Along the road, trees sing to themselves.
Paying the bill at the restaurant
I close the faux leather check holder,
two padded walls becoming one.

Monologue for a Peach

When you behold the softness, do you forget the stone?
Though we may share a shade, I'm not sunset.
Look at the roses, of the same family—
how quickly they go. But we can't say why
the wind blows, is anything but its own wound.
Do you notice the scent I'm sentenced with?
Can I be anything but fallen fruit?
Give me another season to see through.

Mother Stays Over

and bends forward to caress my face.
I lie still, a newborn just fallen asleep
so as not to wake us from this moment.

Last Audition

all the television shows
are bad or dead
and my teeth aren't
straight or white
smile for the camera
with blinders
please slate your name
become a character
if not for the crown
good language
and representation
I will be the lawyer
you can trust
with all your emotions
down to the last draft
my agent says
things will get better
if not now then soon
very soon
as the palm trees
always sunny
wave in the wind
to further my practice

I look away
from the screen
turn up the volume
of someone deemed
the type to die
what do you hear
in this game of girls
I'm breaking cards
master of walking away

Season 4

There Is an Opening

The river moves
from one place to another.
Immigrant, overflowing
with what we can't name
in just a single word:
cup full, braid undone.
Your words roll with mine
so that we don't know
where we began
and where we'll end,
two places at once.
The poem is a tributary
in which I swim
toward other poems,
the light on the water,
the sound of an opening.
The river shows me the way.
I can feel it as we speak.

Frame

I was a child who never played house (the game of family, kitchen, kids)

Just the house. Halved was a window through which I escaped.

When I stepped out of the frame

I saw everything no longer square my own air. The poem is the rain around it.

What I'm trying to say is

the feeling's the frame my words a river that meets the rain.

Returning to Austin

1.

I hum along
with the live music
of creeks trickling
through my veins,
not like the rivers
of other cities
that did not sing
of my childhood.
Just above ground,
limestone frame.
The trees in me
recall the weather:
fists of juniper
pollen flooding
like the light,
oak trees reaching
for something bigger,
branches of ash
trying to extinguish
the fever of humidity.
Smoke of all I've tasted,
the heat and the sting.
Clouds float in the river
mirroring the sky.
I've come home
right before the rain.

2.

Strips of rib cut across the grain
soaked in sesame oil, soy sauce,
onion, garlic, and honey
flipped on the grill

rows of oval bones
scrolls seared in the brain.
Fried egg smooth as a mother
dolsot bibimbap mixed

kimchi jjigae bubbling
orange-red in stone bowls.
Cloud of purple rice
cradled in romaine

spoon in gochujang
like brush to paint,
nine squares of banchan
a rainbow over the table.

This is where I arrive hungry
with friends with family
and leave fulfilled
every dish and bowl cleared.

Nothing else needs to be said,
the receipt's tongue listing
everything we all insist
we'll take care of.

3.

I remember my brother
driving me around

through old Austin
windows down

when the high
was only in the 90s

an armadillo
crossing the road

and we'd get there
in a quarter of the time

it takes these days
with the rest of the line

less scraping of the sky
listening to both sides

of the cassette recorded
between episodes

before I pressed stop
cut him out of my life

they love me like I was a brother
they protect me, listen to me

the wind and the chords
merging on the highway

the tape connected
from reel to reel

4.

At Barton Springs
in mid-November
someone waist deep
prays to the sun.
Water flows under
hands pressed together.
Blue-green youth,
limestone light,
egret an elegant
question mark.
Past the fence,
tracks of the train
I rode as a kid remain
along with the rocks.
(Still the same ones
or all thrown?)
Rather than sink
in pleasure or grief,
my parents rarely swam.
The heat always
drove me mad.
Skyline's growing
teeth and crown,
but who wants to be king?
Why did I come back?
Gratitude and all that.

5.

At sunset   I join the tourists on the Congress Avenue Bridge   lined up like an accordion

for the performance   leaning on the rails   notes on sheet music   the bats pepper the sky

my brother visiting from D.C.   tried to catch them with my parents   when I was in New York

they waited   but the bats never arrived   it feels like it would be sadder

to watch them with my family   fly away   to see more than a million Mexican free-tailed

bats leave   and then my parents   would have to drive all the way home

the bats glide   along the Colorado River   where exactly we don't know   we don't see

the mothers with their pups   going their separate ways   to feast while we're asleep

returning before dawn   news stations mistaking them   for incoming rain showers

they've been taking flight from here   for more than 40 years

ever since I was born   in this city the bats call home

my mother cuts a grapefruit in half

into a dozen little boats

someday I'll leave   but in the middle of the night   I'll still see you

To Be Seen, To Be Heard

". . . We want to be seen, we want to be heard . . ."
—Michelle Yeoh, 2023 Screen Actors Guild Awards speech

The immigrants given the finger on the subway as it shoots them from Manhattan to Brooklyn

The grandparents' home graffitied, stain on the off-white decaying fence, the do-it-yourself cleanup, translation: a bird did it

The mother who doesn't disclose what happened, remembering how the police stopped her car and asked for her identification

The urge to empty the bladder in an hour of questioning, to be home

The neighbor assaulted in her apartment complex by the girl next door, the inability to return alone

The panel discussion on safety and solidarity in the wake of anti-Asian hate,
hours after the Uvalde shooting, the fatigue in their faces, the work to be there

The friend who shouts back to the catcaller, who in anger doesn't think about death

The victims' photos blown up at the scene of the crime in the days after their deaths

The employee who didn't ask to be called a hero retracing his steps for the news

The actress dedicating her award to *all the little boys and girls who look like me*

The Korean ajummas at the Black Lives Matter rally proclaiming "흑인의 생명은 소중하다": *Black lives are precious*

The son fluent in the language of grief

The lines growing, learning to live together

My Father's Love Language

Is being there early, showing up before me. His hands clasped in prayer as if holding a sparrow singing my mother's song—her name meaning love, for which he and I once wrestled, our raised arms a roof. Eating everything, having once been hungry. Slicing a pineapple, bright bags in my freezer full as a suitcase, and bringing a battery for the secondhand clock he gave me so I won't be alone with the sound of my own silence. Weeping on the flight back to Austin after visiting me in New York, which my mother tells me. Healing her shoulder the way her father did, saying, *Health is most important in our life.* Writing, *You are doing better than I was at your age.* When I send him a picture of the snow in my mountain town he marvels at the *snow covered scenery.* I remember the *snow covered hills* of Fleetwood Mac's "Landslide" and, at three, my first time seeing snow with him in our front yard. Does he know that song? Our words growing as we get older. Abbreviating my name to Dia.!, a day of joy where a daughter lives. A letter that ends *With love.*

Living Together

The orchid buds are pistachios
coming out of their shells,
fists uncurling. Mouths open
one by one along the stem,
butterflies hanging on for dear life,
dear light growing in a new room.
My love grinds coffee like ashes
blooming from this cup.

Living with you is living twice,
the same person born again
lying side by side in the womb.
For a moment we only hear each other—
not the cars passing on the street,
not even the hyenas below us.
Your hand laced with mine,
ears pressed together
like wings, halves of a heart.

Not Quite the Apocalypse

the last of the poets carry

teacups through the din

and the dust dodging rocks

as the scaffolding rises

search for that last

folded sheet of paper

after looking to the side

at extinct birds and trees

they make their way forward

porcelain falling to pieces so small

they can't be broken further

ready to hide in a pocket

shattered so much that they

no longer need to be explained

no longer can explain

Visiting the Ucross Chapel

Clearmont, Wyoming

I came to see the rocks that make up the church of my life
the stones that don't touch anymore   the dog
walking around it   the light looks different now
making the frame that much clearer
two doors side by side a prayer
the deer look up from the grass
as they open   startle at the sight
of beauty   flicker of white tail
a moment of peace
through the house's eyes   the sun
washing over all it has seen
alone among the pews   a cloud
of breath   the sky   stained glass
two trees waiting for a bell to ring
pine's umbrella gesturing to the horizon
I close my eyes and make a wish for the world
congregation of trees   chorus of birds
though I doubt it will ever come true
I do it anyway   for another glimpse
of patience   something that stays

On Their First Date

My parents walk hand in hand through the snow in Seoul.
Instead of flowers, my dad brings a dozen doughnuts.
As fires burn halfway around the world.

Connect the dots between each falling flake.
My brothers and I were born, making five of us—
a star, a line that returns to where it began.

The way to a woman's heart is through her stomach,
through her hopes and dreams, a hole.
She belly laughs when he pops through the open roof
of the bus that won't hold his whole frame.

Crumbs of snow we hold onto to keep the path clear,
subtitles accumulating as they embrace.

How to Cast a Beautiful Animal

Fame was a name I confused with form.

To be contained by nothing but one.

Instead of trying to fit into the frame

I cast myself, a mosaic of screens,

all the pieces of the game.

An endless sleep full of dreams,

a performance never recorded.

One day I woke, remembered the lines

that were my life. And I spoke.

Acknowledgments

Thanks to the editors of the following publications, where versions of these poems first appeared:

The Asian American Literary Review: "Artemisia," "Han," "Not Quite the Apocalypse"

The Atlas Review: "Self-Portrait as Asian American Actress" ["In high school plays..."]

Barrow Street: "My Brother Was My Father"

Boston Review: "The One"

The Common: "On Their First Date"

The Common Online Monthly Poetry Feature: "Living Alone," "Living Together"

Denver Quarterly: "American Anagrams," "First Language," "grief"

diode: "Ferment," There Is an Opening"

Duende: "At the Wheel"

Hayden's Ferry Review: "Spirals I Have Admired"

Hobart: "Ode to the '90s"

The Journal: "In the Morning Light"

The New Republic: "Neighborhood Watch"

Ninth Letter: "1984"

Pleiades: "Self-Portrait as Asian American Actress" ["Red lips, red dress..."]

Portland Review: "Say Something About Yourself"

Prairie Schooner: "Self-Portrait as Asian American Actress" ["In the city of angels..."]

Prelude: "Lessons in Korean," "Office Sun"

Southern Indiana Review: "Country Dinner Playhouse," "Land of the Morning Calm"

TINGE: “Naming These Things,” “Monologue for a Peach”
Vinyl: “Pearl & Ash”
wildness: “Anniversary,” “Two Suitcases and a Map”
Witness: “Visiting the Ucross Chapel”

Many poems also appear in the chapbook *At the Reel*, selected by Tomás Q. Morín as the winner of a Poetry Society of America Chapbook Fellowship.

Thank you to Richard Morrison and Fordham University Press, and to Poetic Justice Institute Prizes Series Editor Elisabeth Frost and JoAnne McFarland for selecting my manuscript.

Thank you to MacDowell, the Fine Arts Work Center, Ucross Foundation, Yaddo, Willapa Bay AiR, and I-Park for their support.

Thank you to my teachers, including Khaled Mattawa, Judith Kroll, Erica Wright, Monica Youn, Marcus Wicker, Yanyi, and NYU faculty Charles Simic, Major Jackson, Matthew Rohrer, Eileen Myles, Yusef Komunyakaa, and Sharon Olds. Thanks also to Cathy Park Hong and Cynthia Arrieu-King.

Thank you to my partner for the kindness and laughter.

Thank you to my parents for their encouragement and love.

Diana Keren Lee is the winner of a Poetry Society of America Chapbook Fellowship and a National Poetry Series finalist. Her work has appeared in *Boston Review*, *Denver Quarterly*, *The New Republic*, *Pleiades*, *wildness*, and elsewhere.

POETIC JUSTICE INSTITUTE

Diana Keren Lee

How to Cast a Beautiful Animal

T. S. Leonard

Another Anthem of Fabulous Survival

foreword by Meg Day

Adedayo Agarau

The Years of Blood

Marcella Durand

A Winter Triangle

foreword by Srikanth Reddy

POETS OUT LOUD

Prize Winners

Jennifer Atkinson, *A Gray Realm the Ocean*
Alison Powell, *Boats in the Attic*
Stephanie Ellis Schlaifer, *Well Waiting Room*
Sarah Mangold, *Her Wilderness Will Be Her Manners*
José Felipe Alvergue, *scenery: a lyric*
S. Brook Corfman, *My Daily Actions, or The Meteorites*
Henk Rossouw, *Xamissa*
Julia Bouwsma, *Midden*
Gary Keenan, *Rotary Devotion*
Michael D. Snediker, *The New York Editions*
Gregory Mahrer, *A Provisional Map of the Lost Continent*
Nancy K. Pearson, *The Whole by Contemplation of a Single Bone*
Daneen Wardrop, *Cyclorama*
Terrence Chiusano, *On Generation & Corruption*
Sara Michas-Martin, *Gray Matter*
Peter Streckfus, *Errings*
Amy Sara Carroll, *Fannie + Freddie: The Sentimentality of Post–9/11 Pornography*
Nicolas Hundley, *The Revolver in the Hive*
Julie Choffel, *The Hello Delay*
Michelle Naka Pierce, *Continuous Frieze Bordering Red*
Leslie C. Chang, *Things That No Longer Delight Me*
Amy Catanzano, *Multiversal*
Darcie Dennigan, *Corinna A-Maying the Apocalypse*
Karin Gottshall, *Crocus*
Jean Gallagher, *This Minute*
Lee Robinson, *Hearsay*
Janet Kaplan, *The Glazier's Country*
Robert Thomas, *Door to Door*
Julie Sheehan, *Thaw*
Jennifer Clarvoe, *Invisible Tender*

www.ingramcontent.com/pod-product-compliance
Lightning Source LLC
Chambersburg PA
CBHW030342040826
49266CB00030B/348

* 9 7 8 1 5 3 1 5 1 4 3 6 5 *